RANGE & TRANSPOSITION GUIDE

to 250 Musical Instruments

with French, Italian, and German Translations

Compiled & Edited By

Robert G. Bornstein

$2.50

Sole Selling Representative

WESTERN INTERNATIONAL MUSIC, INC.

2859 Holt Avenue, Los Angeles, Calif. 90034

Library of Congress Catalog Card Number: 64-22747

PRINTED IN THE UNITED STATES OF AMERICA

CONTENTS

EXPLANATION OF USE

The semibreve-notes (○) show the <u>practical range</u> of the instrument *in actual sounds*.

The notes shown in crotchet heads (●) are extreme notes which represent the following:

    (a) Notes playable by the use of specially adjusted instruments.
    (b) Notes playable according to the ability of individual performers.
    (c) Possible but impractical playing notes.

The extreme notes shown are <u>practical extremes only</u>. Most professional performers, particularly BRASS, can exceed that which is considered practical or even extreme.

Crotchet heads shown in brackets [●] indicate the open notes *(tuning in concert key)* of string instruments.

The square note (■) shows the note that is written to sound middle C. The sole purpose of this note is to show the transposition of the instrument (if any) and <u>in no way is this note related to the instrument's range.</u>

T.C. = Treble-clef   A.C. = Alto-clef

Ten. C. = Tenor-clef   B.C. = Bass-clef

TUNING
(in concert key)

EXAMPLE

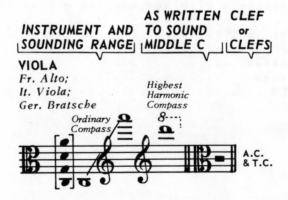

PICCOLOS - FLUTES
FIFE

Db PICCOLO
Fr. Petite Flute en Re b;
It. Ottavino in Re b;
Ger. Kleine Flöte
in Des

T.C.

C FLUTE
Fr. Flute;
It. Flauto;
Ger. Flöte

T.C.

C PICCOLO
Fr. Petite Flute;
It. Ottavino;
Ger. Kleine
Flöte

T.C.

FLAGEOLET (in G)

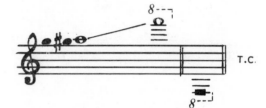

T.C.

Eb SOPRANO FLUTE
Fr. Flute Dessus en Mib;
It. Flauto Soprano in Mib;
Ger. Sopranflöte in Es

T.C.

G ALTO FLUTE
Fr. Flute Alto;
It. Flautone;
Ger. Altflöte

T.C.

BASS FLUTE
Fr. Flute Basse;
It. Flauto Basso;
Ger. Bassflöte

T.C.

FIFE (in Bb - 6 hole)
Fr. Fifre;
It. Piffero;
Ger. Querpfeife

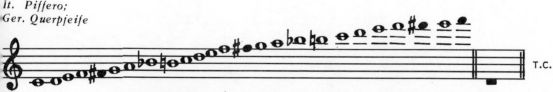

T.C.

(The **KEYED FIFE** in Bb can play the same range *chromatically.*)

DOUBLE REEDS

SOPRANO OBOE in E♭
Fr. Hautbois Dessus en Mi♭;
It. Soprano Oboe in Mi♭;
Ger. Sopran Oboe
in Es

T.C.

HECKELPHON

T

OBOE
Fr. Hautbois;
It. Oboe;
Ger. Oboe

T.C.

BARITONE OBOE (in C)
Fr. Hautbois Bariton;
It. Oboe Baritono;
Ger. Bariton Oboe

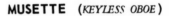

OBOE d'AMORE (in A)
Fr. Hautbois d'Amour

T.C.

MUSETTE *(KEYLESS OBOE)*

ENGLISH HORN (in F)
Fr. Cor Anglais;
It. Corno Inglese;
Ger. Englisches Horn

T.C.

BASSOON
Fr. Basson;
It. Fagotto;
Ger. Fagott

CONTRA BASSOON
Fr. Contrebasson;
It. Contrafagotto;
Ger. Kontrafagott

8---

B.C.

8---

SARRUSOPHONES

These are double-reed, metal instruments that have the Key-mechanism of the saxophone. They were invented in 1856 by the French bandmaster Sarrus, who wanted an additional complete section of voices in French bands. These double-reed instruments have the tone quality of Oboes, English Horns and Bassoons, and can be played with single-reed mouthpieces. However, when single-reed mouthpieces are used, the tenors, altos and sopranos lose a little of their richness and English Horn quality.

B♭ SOPRANO SARRUSOPHONE
Fr. Sarrusophone Dessus en Si♭;
It. Sarrusofone Soprano in Si♭;
Ger. Sopran Sarrusophon in B

E♭ BARITONE SARRUSOPHONE
Fr. Sarrusophone Bariton en Mi♭;
It. Sarrusofone Baritono in Mi♭;
Ger. Bariton Sarrusophon in Es

E♭ CONTRALTO SARRUSOPHONE
Fr. Sarrusophone Contralto en Mi♭;
It. Sarrusofone Contralto in Mi♭;
Ger. Contralt Sarrusophon in Es

B♭ BASS SARRUSOPHONE
Fr. Sarrusophone Basse en Si♭;
It. Sarrusofone Basso in Si♭;
Ger. Bass Sarrusophon in B

B♭ TENOR SARRUSOPHONE
Fr. Sarrusophone Tenor en Si♭;
It. Sarrusofone Tenore in Si♭;
Ger. Tenor Sarrusophon in B

E♭ CONTRA BASS SARRUSOPHONE
Fr. Sarrusophone Contrebasse en Mi♭;
It. Sarrusofone Contrabasso in Mi♭;
Ger. Kontrabass Sarrusophon in Es

C CONTRA BASS SARRUSOPHONE
Fr. Sarrusophone Contrebasse en Ut;
It. Sarrusofone Contrabass in Do;
Ger. Kontrabass Sarrusophon in C

CLARINETS

E♭ CLARINET
Fr. Petite Clarinette en Mi♭;
It. Clarinetto Piccolo in Mi♭;
Ger. Klarinette
in Es

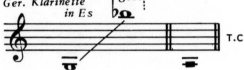

T.C.

B♭ CLARINET
Fr. Clarinette en Si♭;
It. Clarinetto in Si♭;
Ger. Klarinette
in B

D CLARINET
Fr. Clarinette en Re;
It. Clarinetto in Re;
Ger. Klarinette
in D

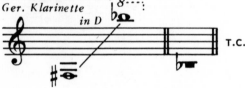

T.C.

A CLARINET
Fr. Clarinette en La;
It. Clarinetto in La;
Ger. Klarinette
in A

C CLARINET
Fr. Clarinette on Ut;
It. Clarinetto in Do;
Ger. Klarinette
in C

T.C.

HECKELCLARIND

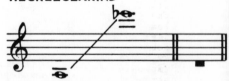

BASSET - HORN (in F)
Fr. Cor de Basset;
It. Corno di Bassetto;
Ger. Bassetthorn

T.C.

A BASS CLARINET
Fr. Clarinette Basse en La;
It. Clarone in La;
Ger. Bass Klarinette in A

T.C.

Eb ALTO CLARINET
Fr. Clarinette Alto en Mib;
It. Clarinetto Alto in Mib;
Ger. Altklarinette in Es

T.C.

Eb CONTRA BASS CLARINET
Fr. Clarinette Contrebasse en Mib;
It. Clarino Contrabasso in Mib;
Ger. Kontrabass
*   Klarinette in Es*

T.C.

Bb BASS CLARINET
Fr. Clarinette Basse en Sib;
It. Clarone in Sib;
Ger. Bass Klarinette in B

T.C.

Bb CONTRA BASS CLARINET
Fr. Clarinette Contrebasse en Sib;
It. Clarino Contrabasso in Sib;
Ger. Kontrabass Klarinette in B

T.C.

SAXOPHONES

E♭ SOPRANINO SAXOPHONE
It. Sassophone Sopranino in Mi ♭

T.C.

C MELODY SAXOPHONE
Fr. Saxophone Melodie en Ut;
It. Sassophone Melodie in Do;
Ger. Saxophon Melodia in C

T.C.

C SOPRANO SAXOPHONE
Fr. Saxophone Dessus en Ut;
It. Sassophone Soprano in Do;
Ger. Sopran Saxophon in C

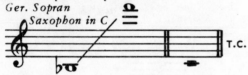

T.C.

B♭ TENOR SAXOPHONE
Fr. Saxophone Tenor en Si ♭;
It. Sassophone Tenore in Si ♭;
Ger. Tenor Saxophon in B

T.C.

B♭ SOPRANO SAXOPHONE
Fr. Saxophone Dessus en Si ♭;
It. Sassophone Soprano in Si ♭;
Ger. Sopran Saxophon in B

T.C.

E♭ BARITONE SAXOPHONE
Fr. Saxophone Bariton en Mi ♭;
It. Sassophone Baritono in Mi ♭;
Ger. Bariton Saxophon in Es

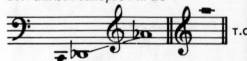

T.C.

E♭ ALTO SAXOPHONE
Fr. Saxophone Haute-Contre en Mi ♭;
It. Sassophone Alto in Mi ♭;
Ger. Alt Saxophon in Es

T.C.

B♭ BASS SAXOPHONE
Fr. Saxophone Basse en Si ♭;
It. Sassophone Basso in Si ♭;
Ger. Bass Saxophon in B

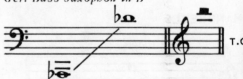

T.C.

TRUMPETS

B♭ PICCOLO TRUMPET
Fr. Petite Trompette en Si♭;
It. Ottavino Tromba in Si♭;
Ger. Kleine Trompete in B

T.C.

C TRUMPET
Fr. Trompette en Ut;
It. Tromba in Do;
Ger. Trompete in C

T.C.

E♭ TRUMPET (*Soprano or Piccolo*)
Fr. Trompette en Mi♭;
It. Tromba in Mi♭;
Ger. Trompete in Es

T.C.

F TRUMPET (*Soprano*)
Fr. Trompette en Fa;
It. Tromba in Fa;
Ger. Trompete in F

T.C.

D TRUMPET
Fr. Trompette en Re;
It. Tromba in Re;
Ger. Trompete in D

T.C.

F TRUMPET (*Alto*)
Fr. Trompette en Fa;
It. Tromba in Fa;
Ger. Trompete in F

T.C.

B♭ TRUMPET
Fr. Trompette en Si♭;
It. Tromba in Si♭;
Ger. Trompete in B

T.C.

continued

10

A TRUMPET
Fr. Trompette en La;
It. Tromba in La;
Ger. Trompete in A

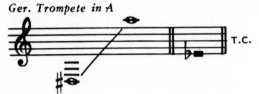

T.C.

D BACH TRUMPET (No valves)

BASS TRUMPET IN C
Fr. Trompette Basse en Ut;
It. Tromba Bassa in Do;
Ger. Basstrompete in C

OR

T.C.
or
B.C.

C BACH TRUMPET (No valves)

BASS TRUMPET IN B♭
Fr. Trompette Basse en Si♭;
It. Tromba Bassa in Si♭;
Ger. Basstrompete in B

OR

T.C.
or
B.C.

COACH HORN (in B♭)

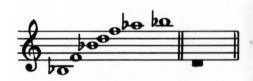

HERALD TRUMPET (in B♭)
(Commonly known as Aida Trumpet)

T.C.

POSTHORN (in A)

CORNETS - FLÜGELHORNS

Eb PICCOLO CORNET
Fr. Petite Cornet en Mib;
It. Ottavino Cornetto or Cornetta in Mib;
Ger. Kleine
Cornett in Es

T.C.

ALTO HORN in Eb (Alto Cornet)
(Eb Alto, *Bell Front or Bell Up*)
Fr. Bugle Alto en Mib;
It. Flicorno Alto in Mib;
Ger. Althorn or Altkornett in Es

T.C.

Bb CORNET
Fr. Cornet en Sib;
It. Cornetto or Cornetta in Sib;
Ger. Cornett in B

T.C.

Eb SOPRANO FLÜGELHORN
Fr. Bugle Dessus en Mib;
It. Flicorno Soprano in Mib;
Ger. Sopran Flügelhorn in Es

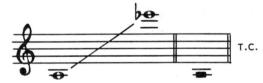

T.C.

A CORNET
Fr. Cornet en La;
It. Cornetto or Cornetta in La;
Ger. Cornett in A

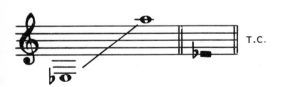

T.C.

Bb FLÜGELHORN
Fr. Bugle en Sib;
It. Flicorno in Sib;
Ger. Flügelhorn in B

T.C.

ALTO HORN in F (Alto Cornet)
Fr. Bugle Alto en Fa;
It. Flicorno Alto in Fa;
Ger. Althorn or Altkornett in F

T.C.

Eb ALTO FLÜGELHORN
Fr. Bugle Haute-Contre (Bugle Alto) en Mib;
It. Flicorno Alto in Mib;
Ger. Alt Flügelhorn in Es

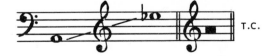

T.C.

BUGLES

Bb BUGLE
Fr. Bugle en Sib;
It. Tromba in Sib;
Ger. Bügelhorn in B

T.C.

KEYED BUGLE IN Bb

T.C

G BUGLE
Fr. Bugle en Sol;
It. Tromba in Sol;
Ger. Bügelhorn in G

T.C.

KEYED BUGLE IN C

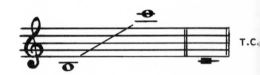

T.C.

BUGLE in G (Slide *(crook)* to F)
Military Regulation

T.C.

KEYED BUGLE IN A

T.C.

SOPRANO PISTON BUGLE in G to D (Rotary Valve to F#)

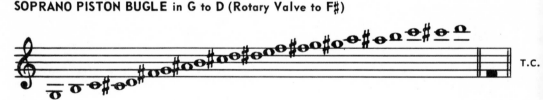

T.C.

SOPRANO PISTON BUGLE in G to D (Rotary Valve to F)

T.C.

SAXHORNS

Invented by Adolphe Sax in 1843 by the application of the valve-mechanism to *Keyed-Bugles* and *Ophicleides*.

E♭ SOPRANINO SAXHORN
Fr. Petite Saxhorn, Petite Bugle á Pistons en Mi♭;
Ger. Piccolo in Es
✳ (E♭ Piccolo Cornet, pg *11*)

T.C.

B♭ TENOR SAXHORN
Fr. Baryton en Si♭;
Ger. Tenorhorn in B, Bassflügelhorn
✳ (Baritone in B♭, *Tenor Horn*, pg *17*)

T.C.

B♭ SOPRANO SAXHORN
Fr. Contralto Saxhorn en Si♭;
Ger. Flügelhorn in B
✳ (B♭ Cornet, pg *11*)

T.C.

B♭ BASS SAXHORN
Fr. Tuba Basse en Si♭;
Ger. Euphonium, Baryton, Tenorbass in B
✳ (Euphonium, pg *17*)

T.C.

E♭ ALTO SAXHORN
Ger. Althorn in Es
✳ (Alto Horn, *Alto Cornet*, pg *11*)

T.C.

E♭ BASS SAXHORN
Fr. Bombardon en Mi♭
✳ (E♭ Military Tuba, pg *17*)

T.C.

B♭ CONTRA BASS SAXHORN
Fr. Bombardon en Si♭;
Ger. Kontrabasstuba in B
✳ (BB♭ Military Tuba, pg *17*)

T.C.

✳ This denotes the contemporary counterpart.

FRENCH HORN in B♭
Fr. Cor-a-pistons en *Sib;*
It. Corno Ventile in *Sib;*
Ger. Ventilhorn in B

T.C.
& B.C.

FRENCH HORN in E♭
Fr. Cor-a-pistons en *Mib;*
It. Corno Ventile in *Mib;*
Ger. Ventilhorn in Es

T.C.
& B.C.

FRENCH HORN in F
Fr. Cor-a-pistons en *Fa;*
It. Corno Ventile in *Fa;*
Ger. Ventilhorn in F

T.C.
& B.C.

DOUBLE HORN (in B♭ & F)

T.C.
& B.

MELLOPHONE in E♭ (E♭ Alto, *Coiled*)
(CONCERT HORN)

T.C.

COR de CHASSE in E♭ (NATURAL HORN)

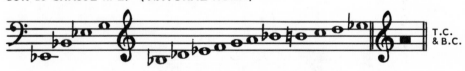

T.C.
& B.C.

(Also, in D)

TUBEN
(Wagner Tubas)

TENOR TUBEN in B♭

BASS TUBEN in F

T.C.
or
B.C.

Modified Horns

CONTRA BASS TUBA

B.C.

This is the four-valve Tuba that was intro-
duced by Wagner to complete the group of so-
called "Wagner Tubas" which was comprised
of two high and two low *Modified Horns* and
one true Tuba.

TROMBONES

SOPRANO TROMBONE (in B♭)
(Slide Trumpet)

T.C.

ALTO TROMBONE (in E♭)
Fr. Trombone Haute-Contre en Mi♭;
It. Trombone Alto in Mi♭;
Ger. Altposaune in Es

A.C.
B.C.
& T.C.

TENOR TROMBONE (in B♭)
Fr. Trombone Tenor;
It. Trombone Tenore;
Ger. Tenorposaune

B.C.
&
Ten.C.

BASS TROMBONE in B♭
Fr. Trombone Basse en Si♭;
It. Trombone Basso in Si♭;
Ger. Bassposaune
in B

B.C.
&
Ten.C.

BASS TROMBONE in G
Fr. Trombone Basse en Sol;
It. Trombone Basso in Sol;
Ger. Bassposaune
in G

B.C.

BASS TROMBONE in F
Fr. Trombone Basse en Fa;
It. Trombone Basso in Fa;
Ger. Bassposaune
in F

B.C.

BASS TROMBONE in E♭
Fr. Trombone Basse en Mi♭;
It. Trombone Basso in Mi♭;
Ger. Bassposaune
in Es

B.C.

CONTRA BASS TROMBONE (in B♭)
Fr. Trombone Contrebasse;
It. Trombone Contrabasso;
Ger. Kontrabass
Posaune

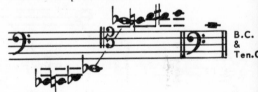

B.C.

VALVE TROMBONE (in B♭) (3 valve)
Fr. Trombone a Pistons;
It. Trombone Ventile;
Ger. Ventilposaune

B.C.
&
Ten.C

VALVE TROMBONE (in B♭)
(7 cylinder)

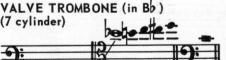

B.C.
&
Ten.C

TUBAS

BARITONE (in B♭) (3 valves)
Fr. Bugle Ténor en Si♭,
    Baryton en Si♭;
It. Flicorno Tenore in Si♭;
Ger. Tenorhörn in B

ORCHESTRA TUBA (in F)

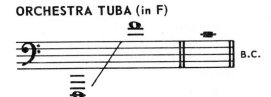

EUPHONIUM (in B♭) (4 valves)
Fr. Basse 'a Pistons;
It. Eufonio;
Ger. Baryton

E♭ MILITARY TUBA

(Helicon, Sousaphone)

BB♭ & CC MILITARY TUBA

(Helicon, Sousaphone)

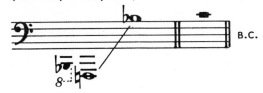

18

PERCUSSION

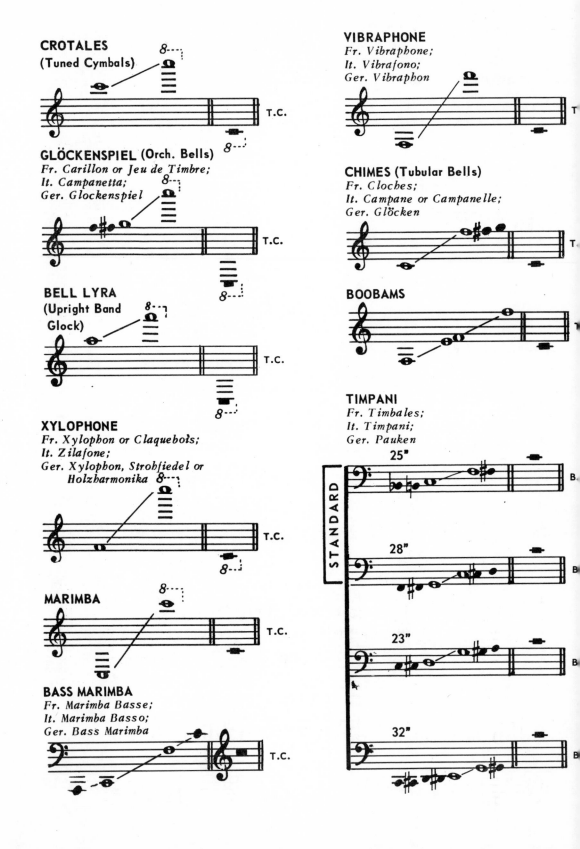

GUITARS

GUITAR (Spanish, Classic)
Fr. Guitare;
It. Chitarra;
Ger. Guitarre

T.C.

(The same tuning is used for Dance-Band Electric Guitar.)

STEEL GUITAR (Hawaiian)

T.C.

GUITAR (12 string)

T.C.

GUITAR
(Special Electric with coupling device for extended range)

T.C.

ALTO GUITAR (in F)
Fr. Guitare Haut-Contre;
It. Chitarra Alto;
Ger. Alt Guitarre

T.C.

TIPLE (in G)

T.C.

PORTUGESE GUITAR in E♭ (12 string)

T.C.

BASS GUITAR (6 string electric)
Fr. Guitare Basse;
It. Chitarra Basso;
Ger. Bass Guitarre

T.C.

BASS GUITAR (4 string - also known as "Electric Bass")
Fr. Guitare Basse;
It. Chitarra Basso;
Ger. Bass Guitarre

B.C.

GUITARRON
(Mexican Bass Guitar)

B.C.

LUTAR or GITUTE
(Sometimes known as the 6 STRING LUTE)

T.C.

BANJOS

BANJO (5 string)

PLECTRUM BANJO

TENOR BANJO

CONVENTIONAL LONG-NECK BANJO
(Folk Style - 5 string)

EXTRA LONG - NECK BANJO
(Folk Style - 5 string)

UKULELES

UKULELE (Standard)

There are several methods of tuning, but this is the most common.

TENOR & BARITONE UKULELES

CAVAQUINHO (Brazilian Ukulele)
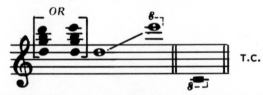

MANDOLINS

MANDOLIN
Fr. Mandoline;
It. Mandolino;
Ger. Mandoline
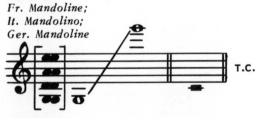

OCTAVE MANDOLA

MANDOLA
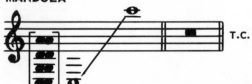

MANDOCELLO

BALALAIKAS

PRIMA BALALAIKA

T.C.

ALTO BALALAIKA

T.C.

SECUNDA BALALAIKA
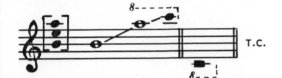
T.C.

BASS BALALAIKA

B.C.

CONTRA BASS BALALAIKA

B.C.

DOMRAS

(Note: A 4th string is sometimes added, tuned a 4th lower than the lowest string.)

PICCOLO DOMRA

T.C.

BARITON DOMRA

T.C.

PRIMA DOMRA

T.C.

BASS DOMRA

B.C.

ALTO DOMRA
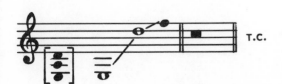
T.C.

CONTRA BASS DOMRA

B.C.

STRINGS

VIOLIN
Fr. Violon;
It. Violino;
Ger. Violine or Geige

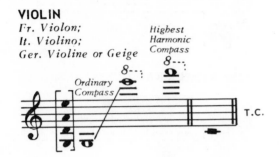

T.C.

CELLO
Fr. Violoncelle;
It. Violoncello;
Ger. Violoncell

B.C.
Ten.C
& T.C

VIOLA
Fr. Alto;
It. Viola;
Ger. Bratsche

A.C.
& T.C.

STRING BASS (Double Bass)
Fr. Contre Basse;
It. Contrabasso;
Ger. Kontrabass

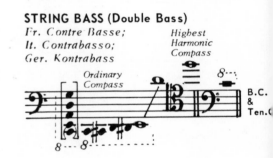

B.C.
&
Ten.C

VIOLA d'AMORE
Fr. Viole d'Amour;
Ger. Liebesgeige

A.C.
& T.C.

KEYBOARD INSTRUMENTS

PIANO
Fr. Piano, Pianoforte;
It. Piano, Pianoforte;
Ger. Klavier, Pianoforte

ACCORDION-Standard *(Chord Buttons-*
(Maj.-Min.-Dom. 7th-Dim.)
Fr. Accordeon;
It. Accordeon;
Ger. Accordeon, Akkordion or Ziehharmonika

ELECTRIC PIANO

ACCORDION - Free Bass System
(No Chord Buttons)

CELESTA

MUSETTE ACCORDION
Fr. Musette Accordeon;
It. Musette Accordeon;
Ger. Musette Accordeon

NOVACHORD

BASS ACCORDION
Fr. Accordeon Basse;
It. Accordeon Basso;
Ger. Bass Accordeon

CONCERTINA

continued

24

HARPSICHORD (Bach Model, *double keyboard*)
Fr. Clavecin;
It. Arpicordo, Clavicembalo;
Ger. Kielflügel

The 16', 8' and 4' stops can be used individually, simultaneously, or coupled in any combination.

SMALL HARPSICHORD (*single keyboard*)
Fr. Petite Clavecin;
It. Ottavino Arpicordo,
   Ottavino Clavicembalo;
Ger. Kleine Kielflügel

The keyboard (8') and 4' stops can be coupled or used individually.

CLAVICHORD
Fr. Clavicorde;
It. Clavicordo;
Ger. Klavichord, Klavier

CALLIOPE

(*This instrument is not manufactured to particular specifications.*)

CLAVIETTA

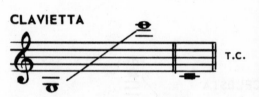

This instrument has a mouthpiece and piano-type keyboard.

VIBRACHORD®
& HARP CELESTE (Maas-Rowe)

The tone selector of the Vibrachord® varies the tone coloring in the amplifier to give a variety of effects. The Harp Celeste, which has no tone selector, has a straight Vibraharp tone.

SOLOVOX

The Bass (32'), Tenor (16'), Contralto (8') and Soprano (4') controls can be used individually, simultaneously, or coupled in any combination.

ORGANS

Note: The following Organ range notations represent the *written ranges only.* The possible sounding ranges are obtained by using the available stops of the particular instrument.

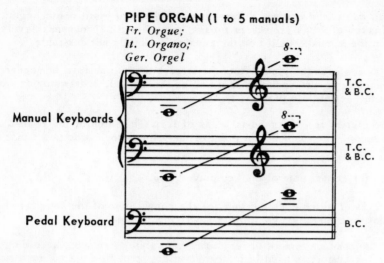

PIPE ORGAN (1 to 5 manuals)
Fr. Orgue;
It. Organo;
Ger. Orgel

Manual Keyboards

T.C. & B.C.

T.C. & B.C.

Pedal Keyboard   B.C.

NAMES OF THE MANUAL KEYBOARDS

The Manual Keyboards are arranged on the instrument in numerical order, with the 1st Manual being closest to the performer.

2 Manual	FRENCH	ITALIAN	GERMAN
1st man. Great	I Grand orgue	I Principale	I Hauptwerk
2nd man. Swell	II Positif ou récit	II Organo di coro	II Brustwerk
			Positiv *or* Schwellwerk, *or:*
			I Positiv
			II Hauptwerk
3 Manual			
1st man. Choir (Ch.)	I Grand orgue	I Organo di coro	I Hauptwerk
2nd man. Great (Gt.)	II Positif	II Principale	II Positiv
3rd man. Swell (Sw.)	III Récit	III Organo d'espressione	III Schwellwerk; *or:*
	I Positif		I Rückpositiv
	II Grand orgue		II Hauptwerk
	III Récit		III Brustwerk; *or*
			I Brustwerk
			II Hauptwerk
			III Oberpositiv
4 Manual			
1st man. Choir	I Grand orgue	I Organo di coro	I Brustwerk
2nd man. Great	II Positif	II Principale	II Hauptwerk
3rd man. Swell	III Récit	III Organo d'espressione	III Positiv
4th man. Solo	IV Solo	IV Organo d'assolo	IV Schwellwerk; *or:*
	I Ruckpositif		I Rückpositiv
	II Grand orgue		II Hauptwerk
	III Positif		III Oberwerk
	IV Récit		IV Brustwerk; *or:*
			I Hauptwerk
			II Positiv
			III Schwellwerk
			IV Solowerk
5 Manual			
1st man. Choir	I Grand choeur	I Principale	I Hauptwerk
2nd man. Great	II Grand orgue	II Organo di coro	II Brustwerk
3rd man. Swell	III Bombarde	III Organo d'espressione	III Schwellwerk
4th man. Solo	IV Positif	IV Organo d'assolo	IV Solowerk
5th man. Echo	V Recit	V Organo d'eco	V Echowerk

(NOTE: The manual arrangement of the 5-manual organ varies in different countries and schools.)

continued

WRITTEN ORGAN REGISTRATIONS

In writing for the organ, due to the extreme differences in individual instruments, registration beyond the general classes of stops (shown in italics, pgs 27 and 28), dynamic levels, and pitches other than 8' on the manuals, or 16' on the pedals, is usually not desirable.

A register (stop) is a series of organ pipes, from the largest to the smallest, homogeneous in timbre and intensity, each pipe corresponding to a key on the manual. A drawstop or stop-key on the console brings the series into play.

The relative pitch of registers is expressed in terms of feet. The pitch of the eight foot (8') register is that of the piano. The fundamental pitch of the manual-keyboards is 8'; that of the pedal-keyboard is 16'.

A unison stop produces the normal note of the key played, e.g. 32', 16', 8', 4', 2', 1'.

A mutation stop is a register which does not produce the normal note of the key played, but a natural harmonic of that note, used for creating or modifying timbre.

The mixture ranks are the combinations of upper harmonics, varying in number according to the number of ranks used. The number is usually indicated on the stop. Because of the almost inaudible high pitch of the harmonics of the upper notes, manufacturers must make special modifications after a certain point on the keyboard. These modifications are known as 'breaks' or 'returns', and are made at the discretion of the individual manufacturer.

CHART OF UNISON AND MUTATION STOPS

STOP in feet	Pitch in relation to the note played	32'	16'	8'	4'	2'	1'
				HARMONIC SERIES			
32'	two octaves lower	1st					
16'	one octave lower	2nd	1st				
10 2/3'	a perfect fourth lower	3rd					
8'	normal pitch of note played	4th	2nd	1st			
*6 2/5'	a major third higher	5th					
5 1/3'	a perfect fifth higher	6th	3rd				
*4 4/7'	a harmonic seventh higher	7th					
4'	one octave higher	8th	4th	2nd	1st		
*3 1/5'	one octave and a third higher		5th				
2 2/3'	one octave and a fifth higher		6th	3rd			
*2 2/7'	one octave and a harmonic seventh higher		7th				
2'	two octaves higher		8th	4th	2nd	1st	
1 3/5'	two octaves and a third higher			5th			
1 1/3'	two octaves and a fifth higher			6th	3rd		
*1 1/7'	two octaves and a harmonic seventh higher			7th			
1'	three octaves higher			8th	4th	2nd	1st

* Rare.

The tremolo or tremulant causes a pulsation in the wind supply to the pipes associated with a specific manual-keyboard, thus producing a vibrato effect. Separate tremolos are provided for each manual-keyboard.

The manual-keyboards can be coupled together or to the pedal-keyboard. These are known as manual and pedal couplers. They may be at 8' (unison), 4' (octave), or 16' (sub-octave) pitches on the manuals, and 8' and 4' pitches on the pedals.

The Swell-Pedal activates a shutter on the pipe enclosure, creating a controlled crescendo or diminuendo. There may be separate Swell-Pedals for each manual-keyboard.

The Register Crescendo Pedal gradually brings into play all of the registers, from the softest to the full power of the instrument, overriding the drawstop or stopkey controls. The Sforzando Reversible thumb or toe piston instantly brings into play the full power of the instrument, overriding the drawstop or stopkey controls, and remaining effective until pushed a second time.

STOPS IN COMMON USE

MANUAL STOPS

Foundation Stops (French: *Fonds*) include Principals (Diapasons), Flutes and String stops of unison pitches, all of which are voiced toward the Principal timbre, the characteristic sound of the concert pipe organ which resembles somewhat the orchestral unison of French Horn *mf*, Trombone in cup mute *mf*, Bassoon *p*, and Bass Flute *f*, all sounding middle C.

Principal (Open Diapason) (French: *Montre, Prestant;* German: *Prinzipal;* Italian: *Principale)* *mf-f* 16', 8', 4'; Quint *mf-f* 5-1/3'; Octave *mf-f* 4'; Twelfth *mp-f* 2-2/3'; Fifteenth or Super-Octave *mp-f* 2'; Sifflet or Siffote *mf* 1'; Dulciana or Dolce *pp-mp* 16', 8', 4', 2-2/3', 2'.

Mixture (French: *Mixture, Fourniture, Plein Jeu, Cornet;* German: *Mixtur, Scharf, Kornett, Zimbel;* Italian: *Ripieno*) *mf-ff* 2 to 7 ranks (usually expressed in Roman numerals), usually 3 to 4 ranks and of Principal timbre. The above stops are used in combination to build the Principal or Diapason Chorus, the basic organ sound.

Chorus Reeds (French: *Anches*): Trumpet *f-ff* 16', 8', 4'; Trompette *f-ff* 16', 8', 4'; Tromba or Trombone or Bombarde or Ophicleide *ff* 16', 8', 4'; Tuba *ff-fff* 16', 8', 4'; Clarion *mf-fff* 4'; Oboe or Hautboy (nonimitative) *mp-f* 8', 4'. As their names indicate, these stops have a muffled to brilliant brassy timbre with extremely rapid incisive attack.

Chorus reeds plus Mixtures are used to build the Reed of secondary Chorus on large concert (and church) organs.

Open Flutes (French: *Flute;* German: *Flote;* Italian: *Flauto*): Flute *p-f* 16', 8', 4', 2', 1'; Flauto Mirabilis *f-ff* 8'; Concert Flute *mf-f* 8'; Melodia *mp-mf* 8'; Hohlflote *mp-f* 8'; Waldflote *mp-mf* 8', 4'; Blockflote *mp-f* 4', 2'; Flute Harmonique *mf-f* 8', 4'; Harmonic Piccolo *mf-f* 2'; Piccolo or Flautino *mp-f* 2'; Spitzflote (has a horn-like edge to timbre) *p-mp* 8', 4'. These stops have a round, open tone somewhat like the orchestral Flute or Recorder.

Stopped Flutes (Stopped Diapasons) (French: *Bourdon;* German: *Gedeckt*): Stopped Flute *p-f* 16', 8', 4', 2'; Chimney Flute (French: *Flute a Cheminee;* German: *Rohrflote, Rohrgedeckt*) *mp-mf* 16', 8', 4', 2'. These stops have hollow flute tone similar to the Ocarina, Panpipes, Slide Whistle, or Cuckoo Call.

Quintadenas or *Quintatens* *mp-f* 16', 8', 4', 2' are a unique organ timbre composed of stopped pipes overblown so as to sound their twelfths as loud as the fundamentals. The nearest orchestral equivalent would be the E Clarinet in its lowest register, played as softly as possible.

Strings (French: *Gambe, Viole;* German: *Geigen*): *pp-f* 16', 8', 4'; Salicional *mp-mf* 16', 8', 4'; Salicet *mp-mf* 4'; Viola da Gamba or Gamba *mp-mf* 8'; Cello or Violone *mf-f* 16', 8'; Viola *mp-mf* 8', 4'; Violina *mp-mf* 4', 2'; Muted Viol or Muted String *pp-p* 8', 4'; Aeoline (the softest stop on any organ) *ppp* 8'. These stops have a bright to extremely keen and thin tone similar to orchestral strings and are slow to respond in attack.

Gemshorn *p-f* 8', 4' and *Erzahler* *mp-mf* 8', 4'. These stops have a hybrid flute-string timbre, and are usually quite prompt in speech.

Celestes: stops tuned slightly sharp or flat so as to produce a wavering or beating ensemble or vibrato effect when combined with a unison stop. They may occur in any of the quieter voices, most commonly as a String or Viol Celeste (French: *Voix Celeste*) 8'; Dulciana Celeste or Unda Maris 8', 4'; Flute Celeste 8'; Gemshorn Celeste 8'; Kleiner Erzahler 8'; Cello Celeste 8'. Muted Strings 8', 4'.

Mutations: usually of Flute timbre: Gross Nasard *mf-f* 5-1/3'; Gross Tierce *mp-f* 3-1/5'; Nasard *mp-f* 2-2/3'; Tierce *p-mf* 1-3/5'; Larigot *p-f* 1-1/3'. These stops are combined with unison stops to add tone color for solo registrations.

continued

Solo Reeds: Clarinet *mp-f* 16', 8'; Krummhorn or Cromorne *mp-f* 8'; Cor Anglais *mf* 8'; Vox Humana *pp-mp* 8'; Oboe (imitative) *mp-mf* 8'; French Horn *mf-f* 8'. These stops are more or less imitative, with the possible exception of the Vox Humana, a stop always used with tremulant, which was intended to evoke the effect of a choir humming nasally.

Percussions: Chimes (tubular bells) (8') range: 2 octaves G3-G5; Harp (8' or 4') or Celesta (4') or Celesta Sub (8') range: 4 octaves C3-C7, metal bars with resonators. These stops are quite similar to the Tubular Chimes and Celesta of the orchestra.

PEDAL STOPS

The pedal stops are similar in quality to manual stops of the same names.

Principal (Open Diapason) mf-ff 32', 16', 8', 4'; Choral Bass *f-ff* 4'; Octave *mf-ff* 8'; Quint *mf-ff* 10-2/3', 5-1/3'; Dulciana *pp-mp* 16', 8'.

Mixtures: 2 to 5 ranks of Principal timbre.

The above stops are used in combination to build the principal Pedal Chorus.

Chorus Reeds: Bombarde *ff-fff* 32', 16', 8', 4'; Trombone *f-ff* 16', 8'; Tromba *f-ff* 8'; Clarion *f-fff* 4'; Bassoon or Fagott *mp-f* 16', 8'.

Open Flutes: Grossflote or Flute *mf-ff* 8', 4'.

Stopped Flutes: Bourdon *mp-ff* 32', 16', 8', 4'; Gedeckt *pp-mf* 16', 8'.

Quintadenas or *Quintatens: mp-f* 32', 16', 8'.

Strings: Violone or Violoncello *mp-f* 32', 16', 8'; Salicional *mp-mf* 16'.

Celestes, Mutations, Solo Reeds and Percussions are usually playable on the pedal keyboard only by coupling from the manual divisions.

THEATER PIPE ORGAN

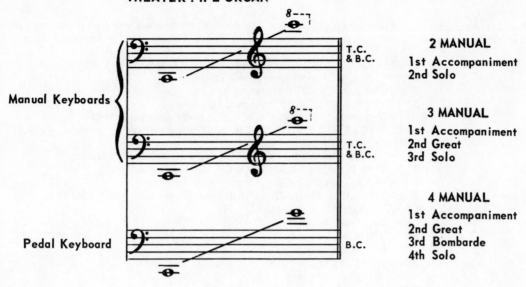

Manual Keyboards

Pedal Keyboard

T.C. & B.C.

T.C. & B.C.

B.C.

2 MANUAL
1st Accompaniment
2nd Solo

3 MANUAL
1st Accompaniment
2nd Great
3rd Solo

4 MANUAL
1st Accompaniment
2nd Great
3rd Bombarde
4th Solo

THEATER PIPE ORGAN

The written and sounding ranges of the Theater Pipe Organ are essentially the same as the Concert Pipe Organ. The essential difference is that a relatively small number of sets or ranks of pipes (registers) are employed, and usually, each is available at a great variety of pitches on all keyboards. These registers are voiced to extreme differences in timbre, and the mutations are derived from the Tibia Clausa (a very heavy stopped flute), and from the Concert Flute (a plain open flute of wood and of moderate intensity).

On the Theater Pipe Organ, the *tremolo* or *vibrato* is most extreme in its action. Separate vibratos are usually provided for the Tibia Clausa, the Vox Humana, the Main or Foundation registers, and the Solo registers. Each register is associated with either the Main or the Solo expression chambers (more in some large instruments); they do not have a 'home' keyboard at the console.

Couplers are held to a minimum, since most registers are already independently available at a great variety of pitches on all keyboards.

Ch.	REGISTERS Name	TIMBRE	PITCHES
S	Tibia Clausa	Stopped Flute *ff*	16', 8', 5-1/3', 4', 2-2/3', 2'
M	Diaphonic Diapason	Principal *ff*	16', 8', 4', (Pedal 32')
S	Horn Diapason	Principal *mf*	16', 8', 4'
M	Concert Flute	Open Flute *mf*	16', 8', 4', 2-2/3', 2', 1-3/5'
S	Solo String	String *f*	16', 8', 4'
S	Solo String Celeste	String *f* (♯)	16', 8', 4'
M	Salicional or Viole d'Orchestre	String *mf*	16', 8', 4', 2
M	Voix Celeste or Viole Celeste	String *mf* (♯)	8', 4'
M	Dulciana	Principal *p*	8', 4'
S	English Horn (Posthorn)	Chorus Reed *ff*	16', 8'
M	Tuba	Chorus Reed *ff*	16', 8', 4'
S	Trumpet	Chorus Reed *f*	16', 8', 4'
S	Saxophone	Solo Reed *mf*	16', 8'
S	Oboe Horn	Solo Reed *mf*	8', 4'
M	Clarinet	Solo Reed *mf*	16', 8'
S	Orchestral Oboe	Solo Reed *mf*	8'
S	Kinura	Solo Reed *mf*	8'
M	Vox Humana	Solo Reed *p*	16', 8', 4'

Ch. = Chamber
M = Main (Left)
S = Solo (Right)

continued

There are many tuned and non-tuned percussion registers that are composed of the actual orchestral instruments, fitted with electro-pneumatic actions. Those usually encountered are:

CHRYSOGLOTT (4') G3-G7, essentially a Celesta.
HARP (4') C3-C7, a single-stroke Marimba.
MARIMBA (4') C3-C7, reiterating action.
XYLOPHONE (2') C4-C7, reiterating action.
GLOCKENSPIEL (2') G5-C8, single-stroke Orchestra Bells.
ORCHESTRA BELLS (2') G5-C8, reiterating action.
CHIMES (8') G3-G5.
PIANO, with Mandolin Effect, (16', 8', 4'), standard compass.
TUNED SLEIGH BELLS (8') C4-C6, reiterating action.
BASS DRUM, (on Pedal).
KETTLE DRUM, (Bass Drum with continuous roll), (on Pedal).
CRASH CYMBAL, (on Pedal).
CYMBAL, (on Pedal).
SNARE DRUM, (Accomp.).
TOM-TOM, (Accomp.).
TAMBOURINE, (Accomp.).
CASTANETS, (Accomp.)
TRIANGLE, (Great).
WOOD BLOCK, (Accomp.).
SAND BLOCK, (Accomp.).

On some instruments, a large group of sound effects is present, such as: *Auto Horn, Locomotive Whistle, Steamboat Whistle, Siren, Fire Gong, Door Bell, Thunder, Surf, Bird Whistle, Horse's Hoofs, Gong, Grand Crash* or *Crockery Smash, Wind,* etc. These are usually controlled by thumb or toe buttons, independent of the keyboards.

The Swell-Pedals have a much more extreme effect on the volume of the Theater Pipe Organ than on the concert (church) instrument. Two Swell-Pedals are usually provided, one each for the Solo (S) and Main (M) chambers.

A Register Crescendo Pedal, which is usually supplied, brings on all the registers from soft to loud, in sequence, overriding the stopkey register controls.

Thumb pistons are provided under each manual keyboard for the rapid changing of registrations for that keyboard. Toe pistons are provided for changing pedal registrations.

ELECTRONIC ORGANS
(other than Hammond Organs)

These instruments have various controls, similar to those found on the Pipe Organ.

Due to the numerous models manufactured to different specifications, the following represents only the '2 manual instruments' that may be most available.

CHURCH & CONCERT MODELS

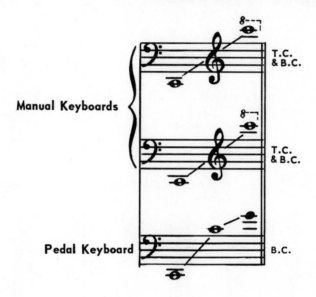

SPINET MODELS

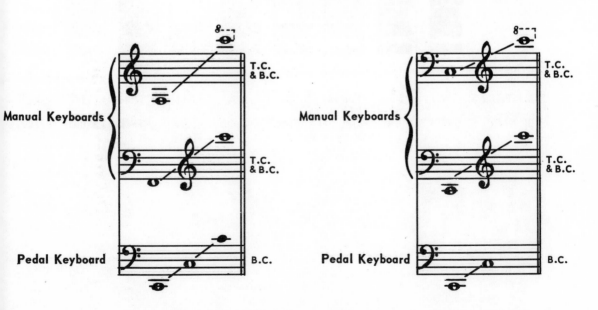

The unique feature of the Hammond Organs is the harmonic drawbar. This device replaces the use of "stops", such as, "diapason", "flute", "strings", etc., and furnishes the fundamentals and harmonics from which these effects and numerous others can be created.

Each harmonic is available in eight stages of intensity (volume), the eight numbers being marked on the drawbars. These numbers are used to indicate the preferred tone qualities so that they can be exactly duplicated when desired.

There are nine drawbars in each group that control the upper and lower manuals of the Console Models. The Spinet Models M-100 and L-100 series have the complete group of nine drawbars that control the upper manual. However, the M-100 series has eight drawbars for the lower manual, and the L-100 series has only seven.

In addition to the manual drawbars, the Console Models have two pedal drawbars. The left drawbar controls the low, deep quality (16 ft. pitch) and the right drawbar adds brightness of tone one octave higher (8 ft. pitch). The Spinet Models have only one pedal drawbar which controls an already combined pedal tone.

The following illustration shows the drawbars in relationship to Pipe Organ terminology.

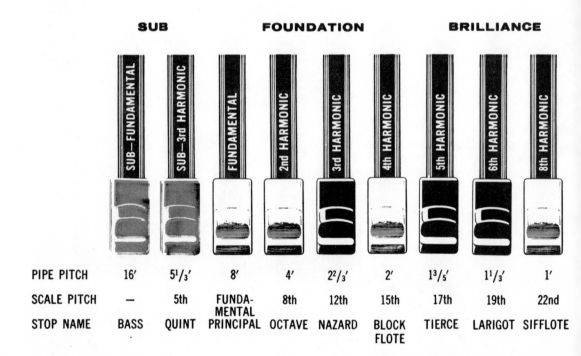

	SUB		FOUNDATION				BRILLIANCE		
	SUB—FUNDAMENTAL	SUB—3rd HARMONIC	FUNDAMENTAL	2nd HARMONIC	3rd HARMONIC	4th HARMONIC	5th HARMONIC	6th HARMONIC	8th HARMONIC
PIPE PITCH	16′	5^1/$_3$′	8′	4′	2^2/$_3$′	2′	1^3/$_5$′	1^1/$_3$′	1′
SCALE PITCH	—	5th	FUNDA-MENTAL	8th	12th	15th	17th	19th	22nd
STOP NAME	BASS	QUINT	PRINCIPAL	OCTAVE	NAZARD	BLOCK FLOTE	TIERCE	LARIGOT	SIFFLOTE

By permission of The Hammond Organ Company

THE COLORS OF THE DRAWBARS

The significance of the colors of the black, white and brown drawbars on the Hammond Organ, is shown in the following illustrations.

CONSONANT

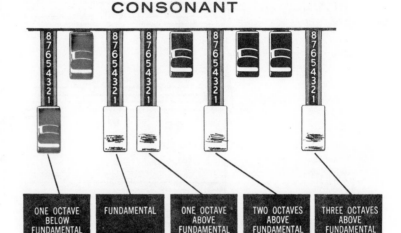

WHITE DRAWBARS

The first white drawbar for each manual represents the fundamental tone. All the other *white* drawbars are octave intervals or harmonics of the fundamental tone. The tonal brilliance is greatly increased by adding white drawbars but the harmonics added are always in 'consonance'.

DISSONANT

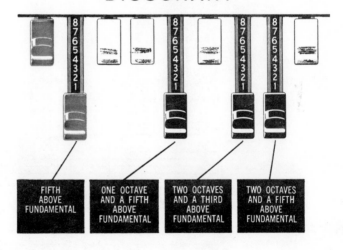

BLACK DRAWBARS

The black drawbars represent the *dissonant* (discordant) harmonics which are also necessary in building rich tone colors. In general, the black drawbars should not be emphasized too strongly above the white drawbars. If a black drawbar is to be emphasized, it is a good rule to use adjacent white drawbars to strengths within two steps of the black drawbar.

By permission of **The Hammond Organ Company**

BROWN DRAWBARS

In addition to the white and black drawbars, there are two brown drawbars. *(These do not exist in the group controlling the lower manual of the Spinet Models.)* These two drawbars produce "sub-octave" effects. The first brown drawbar is the sub-octave of the fundamental and the second brown drawbar is the sub-octave of the third harmonic. These are used to add depth and richness to many combinations. They also increase the range of the keyboard by one octave, since a solo registration for "8 foot", or normal pitch, can be set up using the first brown drawbar as the fundamental, and played one octave higher.

continued

34

HAMMOND CONSOLE MODELS
(Concert Model, Home Model,
C-3 Model & A-100 Series)

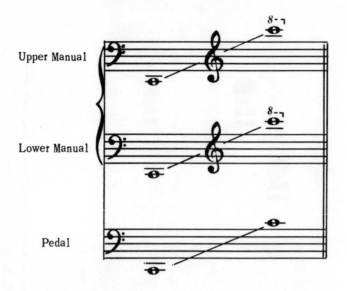

HAMMOND SPINET ORGANS
(Models M-100 & L-100 Series)

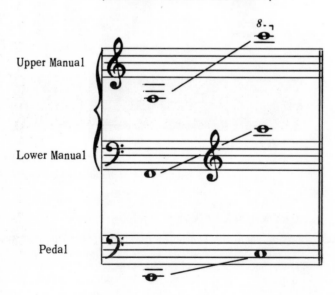

UPPER MANUAL

LOWER MANUAL

In the above illustration you will notice that there are two groups of harmonic drawbars (instead of one) for each manual. The purpose is to allow prepared combinations to be ready and waiting for use. With two groups of drawbars for each manual, it becomes necessary to have control keys (known as *pre-set keys*) to select the group wanted.

There are twelve black and white (*reversed keyboard color*) pre-set keys ranging from C through B. These keys are located to the left of each manual keyboard. The first on each manual is a cancel key. The next nine keys, C♯ through A, are preset to the tones most often used by organists. The last two keys on each manual, A♯ and B (sometimes called "adjust" keys) are actually on-and-off switches to control the tones created and set up on the four groups of drawbars.

The white keys are the solo, and single-tone qualities, the black ones are the ensemble qualities. The softer tones are at the left, gradually growing louder to the right. They are always used one at a time, and *cannot be used in combination.* Pressing one key releases all other keys.

THE CONTROL TABLETS

THE VOLUME AND VIBRATO CONTROLS

There are three control tablets - VOLUME *normal-soft,* VIBRATO SWELL *off-on,* VIBRATO GREAT *off-on,* and a six-position switch

controlling the degrees of VIBRATO (*V-1, V-2, V-3*), and VIBRATO CHORUS (*C-1, C-2, C-3*).

The VIBRATO SWELL tablet turns the VIBRATO or VIBRATO CHORUS *on* or *off* on the "swell" or upper manual. The VIBRATO GREAT does the same on the "great" or lower manual.

PERCUSSION

There are four control tablets - PERCUSSION *on-off,* PERCUSSION VOLUME *soft-normal,* PERCUSSION DECAY *fast-slow,* and PERCUSSION HARMONIC SELECTOR *second-third.*

The position of the HARMONIC SELECTOR tablet determines the pitch at which the percussion tone sounds. When set at *SECOND,* the pitch is up one octave with respect to the Fundamental Drawbar; when set at *THIRD,* the pitch is up an octave and a fifth.

THE SOLO PEDAL UNIT

Exclusive to the Concert Model (RT-3) of the Hammond Organ. This unit augments the 16 ft. and 8 ft. pedal drawbar tones at all pitches:- 32 ft., 16 ft., 8 ft., 4 ft., 2 ft., and 1 ft. A knob controls the volume.

Example of indication for settings of *Pre-Set Keys; Drawbars; Percussion* and *Vibrato* tablets.

UPPER MANUAL:	**(B)** 80 0800 000	PEDAL 54, PERCUSSION: ON, NORMAL, SLOW, SECOND. Vibrato V-3.
LOWER MANUAL:	**A♯** 00 4434 113	

By permission of The Hammond Organ Company

continued

HAMMOND SPINET ORGANS

HARMONIC DRAWBARS
(Model M-100)

LOWER MANUAL   PEDAL   UPPER MANUAL

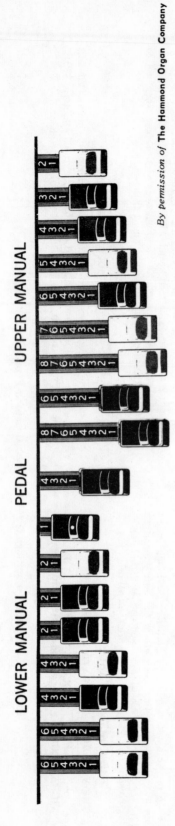

By permission of **The Hammond Organ Company**

Note: The eighth drawbar for the lower manual (*black with white dot*) combines two additional upper harmonics to add richness and brilliance to certain tones.

THE CONTROL TABLETS
(Model M-100)

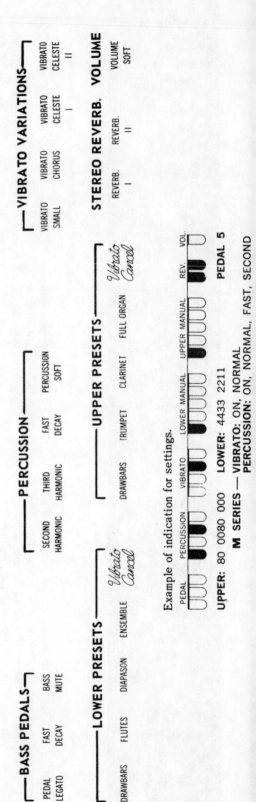

┌─ **PERCUSSION** ┐
SECOND HARMONIC   THIRD HARMONIC   FAST DECAY   PERCUSSION SOFT

┌─ **UPPER PRESETS** ┐
DRAWBARS   TRUMPET   CLARINET   FULL ORGAN   *Vibrato Cancel*

┌─ **BASS PEDALS** ┐
PEDAL LEGATO   FAST DECAY   BASS MUTE

┌─ **LOWER PRESETS** ┐
DRAWBARS   FLUTES   DIAPASON   ENSEMBLE   *Vibrato Cancel*

┌─ **VIBRATO VARIATIONS** ┐
VIBRATO SMALL   VIBRATO CHORUS   VIBRATO CELESTE I   VIBRATO CELESTE II

STEREO REVERB.
REVERB. I   REVERB. II

VOLUME
VOLUME SOFT

Example of indication for settings.

PEDAL   PERCUSSION   VIBRATO   LOWER MANUAL   UPPER MANUAL   REV.   VOL.

UPPER: 80 0080 000   LOWER: 4433 2211   PEDAL 5

M SERIES — VIBRATO: ON, NORMAL
PERCUSSION: ON, NORMAL, FAST, SECOND

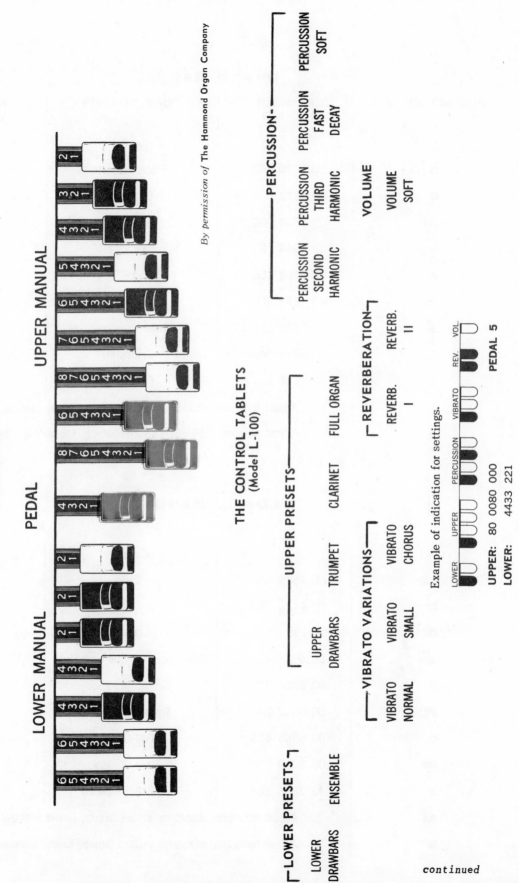

HARMONIC DRAWBARS
(Model L-100)

LOWER MANUAL   PEDAL   UPPER MANUAL

By permission of The Hammond Organ Company

LOWER PRESETS

LOWER DRAWBARS   ENSEMBLE

THE CONTROL TABLETS
(Model L-100)

UPPER PRESETS

UPPER DRAWBARS   TRUMPET   CLARINET   FULL ORGAN

VIBRATO VARIATIONS

VIBRATO NORMAL   VIBRATO SMALL   VIBRATO CHORUS

REVERBERATION

REVERB. I   REVERB. II

PERCUSSION-

PERCUSSION SECOND HARMONIC   PERCUSSION THIRD HARMONIC   PERCUSSION FAST DECAY   PERCUSSION SOFT

VOLUME

VOLUME SOFT

Example of indication for settings.

LOWER   UPPER   PERCUSSION   VIBRATO   REV.   VOL.   PEDAL 5

UPPER: 80   0080   000
LOWER: 4433   221

continued

HAMMOND ORGAN PRE-SET CHART

UPPER MANUAL

PRE-SET KEYS	DRAWBAR SETTING	TONE QUALITY	LOUDNESS VALUE
C		Cancel	
C♯	00 5320 000	Stopped Flute	pp
D	00 4432 000	Dulciana	ppp
D♯	00 8740 000	French Horn	mf
E	00 4544 222	Salicional	pp
F	00 5403 000	Flutes 8' & 4'	p
F♯	00 4675 300	Oboe Horn	mf
G	00 5644 320	Swell Diapason	mf
G♯	00 6876 540	Trumpet	f
A	32 7645 222	Full Swell	ff
A♯	Adjust harmonic drawbars in 1st Group, Upper Manual		
B	Adjust harmonic drawbars in 2nd Group, Upper Manual		

LOWER MANUAL

PRE-SET KEYS	DRAWBAR SETTING	TONE QUALITY	LOUDNESS VALUE
C		Cancel	
C♯	00 4545 440	Cello	mp
D	00 4423 220	Flute & String	mp
D♯	00 7373 430	Clarinet	mf
E	00 4544 220	Diapason, Gamba and Flute	mf
F	00 6644 322	Great, no reeds	f
F♯	00 5642 200	Open Diapason	f
G	00 6845 433	Full Great	ff
G♯	00 8030 000	Tibia Clausa	f
A	42 7866 244	Full Great with 16'	fff
A♯	Adjust harmonic drawbars in 1st Group, Lower Manual		
B	Adjust harmonic drawbars in 2nd Group, Lower Manual		

SOME DISTINCTIVE DRAWBAR REGISTRATIONS
(for all Hammond Organs)

Tibia 16' 72 0020 000	Tibia 8' 00 8240 000	Flute 4' 00 0803 030
Bourdon 16' 54 3100 000	Concert Flute 8' . .00 6421 000	Piccolo 4' 00 0600 000
Diapason 16' 64 3322 000	Diapason 8' 00 5642 110	Octave 4' 00 0545 321
Solo Strings 16' . .25 4421 000	Solo Strings 8' . . .00 2366 542	Solo Strings 4' . . .00 0436 555
Contra Viol 16' . . .24 3210 000	Viol d'Orchestre 8' 00 2444 322	Viol 4' 00 0344 232
Contra Celeste 16'.23 4321 000	Viole Celeste 8' . . .00 2323 211	Octave Celeste 4'. .00 0324 220
Vox Humana 16' . .14 3110 000	Vox Humana 8' . . .00 3400 332	Vox Humana 4' . . .00 0433 042
Oboe Horn 16'. . . .47 5430 000	Oboe Horn 8'. 00 4763 000	Oboe Horn 4' 00 0606 310
Saxophone 16' . . .27 3210 000	Saxophone 8' 00 2478 500	Clarion 4' 00 0515 230
Clarinet 16' 35 2000 000	Clarinet 8' 00 8382 700	Tibia 2'. 00 0006 001
English Horn 16'. .25 3442 100	English Horn 8'. . .00 3577 540	Piccolo 2' 00 0005 111
Ophicleide 16' . . .47 7600 000	Tuba 8' 00 5680 400	Twelfth 00 0060 020

FLUTE TONES

FLUTE TONES
00 6200 000

LIGHT CONCERT FLUTE
00 3700 000

SEVERAL FLUTES TOGETHER
00 7605 004

REED TONES

TYPICAL REED EFFECT
OBOE 00 4632 100

TRUMPET-TYPE TONE
00 6876 540

VOICE-LIKE EFFECT
00 1200 432

CLARINET TONE
00 7272 420

CHORUS REED EFFECT
with sub-octave
76 7777 765

FOUNDATION (Diapason) TONES

PHONON TYPE DIAPASON
00 5521 000

DIAPASON CHORUS
54 5444 222

FULL ORGAN EFFECT
54 7878 766

THEATRE ORGAN EFFECT
87 8766 553 full vibrato

XYLOPHONE TONE
00 0800 080 no vibrato

STRING TONES

VIOLIN TONE
00 4345 554 full vibrato

A STRING SECTION
12 3333 444 string chorus effect

HARMONIUM

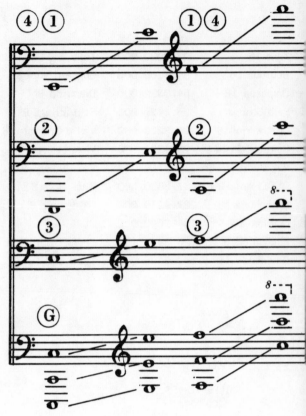

Written Range

T.C. & B.C.

(8')

Note:

The ① of the left hand is for the accompaniment. The ① of the right hand is adapted for light and smooth passages.

①④ = 8'

② = 16'

③ = 4'

REGISTERS OF THE LEFT HAND

⓪	⑤	④	③	②	①
Forte de Basses	Violoncelle	Basson	Clairon	Bourdon	Cor Anglais

MIDDLE REGISTERS

Ⓔⓜ	Ⓖ	Ⓔ
Piano de Basses	Grand Jeu	Expression

REGISTERS OF THE RIGHT HAND

①	②	③	④	⑤	⓪
Flute	Klarinette	Fifre	Hautbois	Musette	Forte des Dessus

CARILLONS

*Carillon music is usually written on two staves, treble and bass clefs.
When the range of the instrument starts from middle C, both staves are
notated in treble clef.*

(Cast Bells)

A Carillon is a set of fixed, cast bells, referred to as *carillonic bells,* that are usually ac-
tivated by a keyboard mechanism. Since there is no set number of cast bells in each Carillon,
a standard range cannot be shown. The playing range can vary from one octave, diatonic, to
four octaves, chromatic, and the performer can control the impact of each strike.

Due to the lack of standardization, it is necessary to check each instrument's sounding range
to determine the key in which the instrument is tuned. The pitch of the Carillon is determined
by the largest (lowest sounding) bell, which is usually called C on the keyboard.

Although harmony can be played on most Carillons, some English carillonic bells are cast
for the sole purpose of being played individually or as units used in change-ringing and the
playing of peals. These bells, sometimes known as *English Pealing Bells,* are not suitable
for playing harmony because of the dissonance of their partial series.

The partial series, sounding from the strike tone of a particular cast bell, may vary according
to individual opinion. However, its basic characteristic is to sound the minor third partial. It
should also be noted that the basic difference between the partial series of a bell-tone and
that of the natural harmonic series is that the partials of the bell-tone sound *below* as well
as *above* the fundamental.

The following shows the partial series (generally accepted) for the harmony-playing English,
Flemish, French, German and American Carillons:

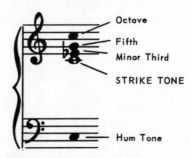

ELECTRONIC CARILLONS

This instrument is an electronic unit with a tone source derived from 25 or more small, solid,
metal rods that are arranged in chromatic sequence. It can be operated by a piano-type keyboard or an automatic playing device.

It should be noted that the resultant tone of an Electronic Carillon differs from that of a cast
bell Carillon. This is explained by the fact that the physical structure of the metal rod makes
it impossible to have an identical series of partials to those of the cast bell. Therefore, a
tuning process is used, and the tuning processes of the partials vary according to the in-
vention of the individual manufacturer.

INSTRUMENT & WRITTEN RANGE　　　*PARTIAL SERIES*

J. C. DEAGAN, INC.

These instruments have *control-
lable dampers* that control the
duration of the ring-time of each
bell tone.

NEW WORLD CARILLON

CANTO-BELL CARILLON

STRIKE TONE sounds 8va basso

continued

MAAS-ROWE CARILLONS

This instrument has an automatic key selector that connects proper major and minor bells to the lower keyboard. This permits playing from one keyboard. On the 122 and 100 bell models, a one-octave pedal-clavier is added for playing the deepest-toned bells.

UPPER (Maj.) KEYBOARD
(Notation: △)
LOWER (Min.) KEYBOARD
(Standard Notation)

SYMPHONIC CARILLON ®

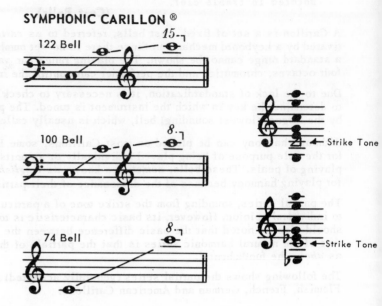

122 Bell

100 Bell

74 Bell

← Strike Tone

← Strike Tone

Due to the subtone (below pitch harmonic), a Carillon tone impresses the ear as sounding one octave lower than played.

STROMBERG-CARLSON COMPANY

The MECHLIN CARILLON has a direct, piano-type action keyboard to create a playing technique similar to that used with a cast bell carillon.

MECHLIN CARILLON

LOUVAIN CARILLON

← Strike Tone

TELEMATICS INC.

This instrument produces the traditional grandeur of the Flemish bells and, at the flick of a switch, the lighter, crisper English bells. A dual keyboard system allows the player to simulate the playing of cast bells. The lower manual hits with the normal intensity of strike and the upper manual has a softer strike.

FLEMISH MASTER CARILLON

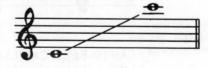

← Strike Tone

SCHULMERICH CARILLONS, INC.

All Schulmerich carillons use precision-tuned, miniature bell-tone generators, struck by metal hammers, as their tone sources. This action duplicates that of a metal clapper striking a cast bronze bell.

The Carillon Americana® Bells are played from a 2 manual organ type console with full pedal clavier built to AGO standards. The 305 Bell instrument is comprised of the following sets of chromatically tuned bells:

- 61 Flemish Bells
- 61 Harp Bells
- 61 Celesta Bells
- 61 Quadra Bells
- 61 Minor Tierce Bells

The Arlington® Carillon has individual expression pedal controls for tenor and treble bells which provide a wide dynamic range for solo and accompaniment.

CARILLON AMERICANA®
Bells Instrument

ARLINGTON® CARILLONS
(Flemish Type)

Multi-toned AMERICANA®
Bells Instruments

These instruments may consist of 2, 3, 4, or 5 octaves of Flemish tuned "Arlington" carillon bells, Harp bells and/or Celesta bells, making it available in 50 to 183 bell ranges. Each set of bells may be manually played from its own respective keyboard, or in combinations from two or more keyboards.

The Coronation® Carillon has a patented Decadence Control which provides the diminishment of tone without a throttling effect of dampers.

CORONATION® CARILLON
(English Type)

HARPS

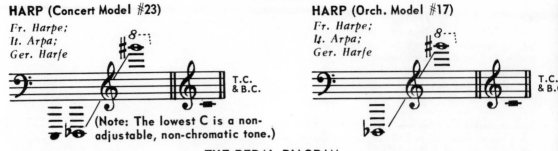

HARP (Concert Model #23)

Fr. Harpe;
It. Arpa;
Ger. Harfe

T.C. & B.C.

(Note: The lowest C is a non-adjustable, non-chromatic tone.)

HARP (Orch. Model #17)

Fr. Harpe;
It. Arpa;
Ger. Harfe

T.C. & B.C

THE PEDAL-DIAGRAM

The vertical lines indicate the positions of the seven transposing pedals which have two notch positions from the neutral position of the key of C♭. The depression of any one pedal into the first notch raises all the strings of its name by one semitone. The depression into the second notch raises them another semitone.

MAJOR CHORD GLISSANDOS

DOMINANT 7th GLISSANDOS

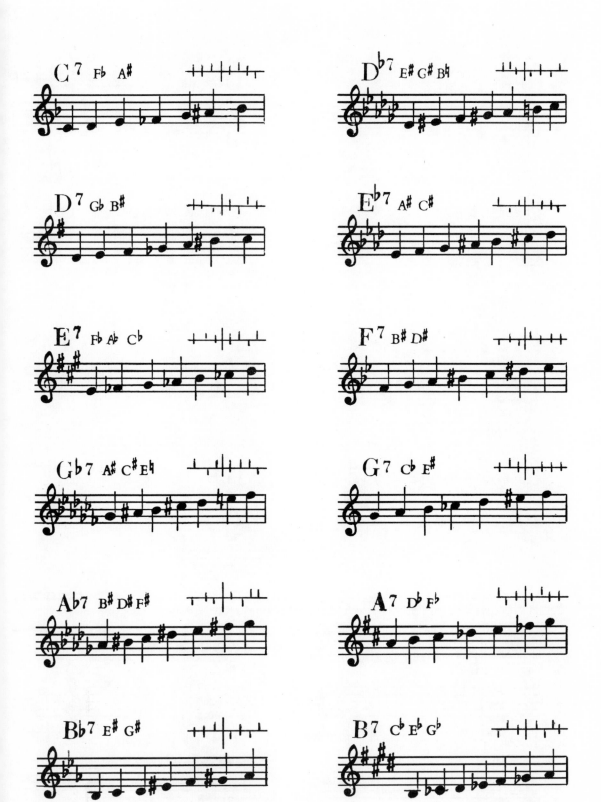

continued

AUGMENTED GLISSANDOS

DIMINISHED 7th GLISSANDOS

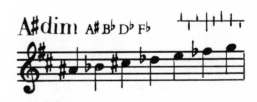

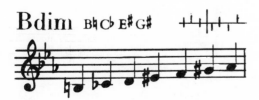

continued

WHOLE TONE SCALES

PENTATONIC SCALE

IRISH HARP

(Note: No pedals. Each string
is hand adjusted ♭ or ♯.)

TROUBADOUR HARP

(Note: No pedals. Each string
is hand adjusted ♭ or ♯.)

OCARINAS

HARMONICAS

Note: These instruments represent the basic group of professional Harmonicas. They are not to be confused with the numerous instruments manufactured in various sizes and keys (chromatic and non-chromatic), usually for amateur or specialized use.

HARMONICA (Standard Chromatic)

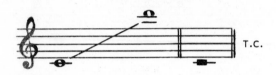

T.C.

HARMONICA (4 Octave Chromatic "64")

T.C.

CHORD HARMONICA (Maj., Min., Dom. 7th, Aug. and Dim. Chords)

CHORD SYMBOLS   T.C.

BASS HARMONICA (Standard)
(Due to limited technical facility, rapid chromatic changes should be avoided.)

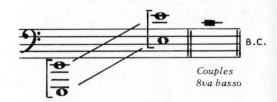

B.C.

Couples
8va basso

BAROQUE & RENAISSANCE INSTRUMENTS

KRUMHORNS (Renaissance Oboes)

CORNETTOS (ZINKES)

SACKBUTS

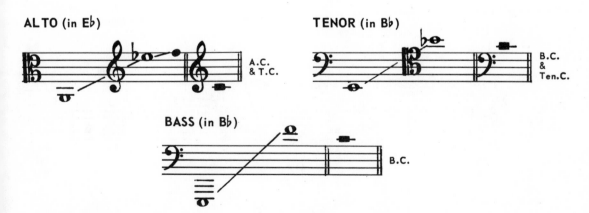

RECORDERS

**NOTE: CHROMATIC INTERVALS ARE
NOT EASILY PLAYED.**

SOPRANINO RECORDER (in F)
Fr. Flûte à Bec Sopranino en Fa;
It. Flauto Dolce, Sopranino in Fa;
Ger. Sopranino Blockflöte in F

TENOR RECORDER
Fr. Flûte à Bec Ténor;
It. Flauto Dolce, Tenore;
Ger. Tenor Blockflöte

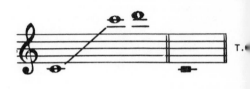

SOPRANO RECORDER (Descant)
Fr. Flûte à Bec Dessus;
It. Flauto Dolce, Soprano;
Ger. Sopran Blockflöte

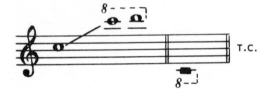

BASS RECORDER (in F)
Fr. Flûte à Bec Basse en Fa;
It. Flauto Dolce, Basso in Fa;
Ger. Bass Blockflöte in F

ALTO RECORDER (in F) (Treble)
Fr. Flûte à Bec Haute-Contre en Fa;
It. Flauto Dolce, Alto in Fa
Ger. Alt Blockflöte in F

GREAT BASS RECORDER (in C)
Fr. Flûte à Bec en Ut;
It. Flauto Dolce, Basso in Ut;
Ger. Gross-bass Blockflöte in C

LUTES

Fr. *Luth;* **It.** *Liuto or Leuto;* **Ger.** *Laute*

The strings of the Lutes are arranged in courses, of which there are 6 basic courses. Almost all modern Lutes are of the "Renaissance" type and they are written for in both "Tablature" and staff notation.

RENAISSANCE LUTES

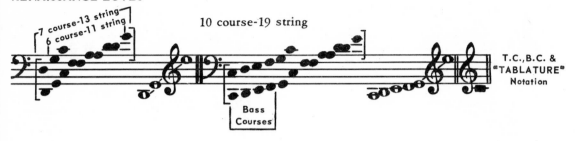

BAROQUE LUTE
12 course-22 string

The full Baroque Lute always has at least 12 courses and 22 strings. They are comprised of the basic 6 courses tuned to the D minor or "Baroque Tuning" (known as the "Nouveau Ton") and 6 or more diatonically tuned bass courses.

VIOLS

Fr. *Viole;* **It.** *Viola;* **Ger.** *Gambe, Kniegeige or Viole*

A family of bowed string instruments which were widely used in the 16th and 17th cent. and have been revived for the performance of music of that period.

DESCANT or TREBLE-VIOL   TENOR-VIOL or VIOLA da BRACCIO

BASS-VIOL or VIOLA da GAMBA

VOICES

OPERATIC

COLORATURA SOPRANO
Fr. Dessus Coloratura;
It. Soprano Coloratura;
Ger. Coloratura Sopran

LYRIC SOPRANO
Fr. Dessus Legere;
It. Soprano di Grazia,
  Soprano Leggiero;
Ger. Lyrischer Sopran

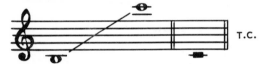

DRAMATIC SOPRANO
Fr. Dessus Dramatique;
It. Soprano Drammatico,
  Robusto, di Forza;
Ger. Heldensopran

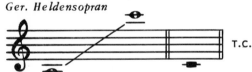

MEZZO SOPRANO
Fr. Bas-Dessus
It. Mezzo Soprano
Ger. Halbsopran

CONTRALTO
Fr. Contralto;
It. Contralto;
Ger. Kontraalt

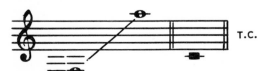

LYRIC TENOR
Fr. Tenor Legere;
It. Tenore di Grazia,
  Tenore Leggiero;
Ger. Lyrischer Tenor

DRAMATIC TENOR
Fr. Tenor Dramatique;
It. Tenore Drammatico,
  Robusto, di Forza;
Ger. Heldentenor

BARITONE
Fr. Baryton;
It. Baritono;
Ger. Baryton, Bariton

BASS BARITONE
Fr. Baryton Basse, Basse-Taille;
It. Baritono Basso;
Ger. Bass Baryton,
Bass Bariton

BASS
Fr. Basse;
It. Basso;
Ger. Bass

ADULT MIXED CHORUS
(Professional Groups)

1st SOPRANO

T.C.

1st TENOR

T.C.

2nd SOPRANO

T.C.

2nd TENOR

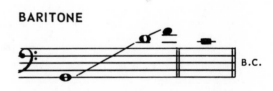

T.C.

1st ALTO

T.C.

BARITONE

B.C.

2nd ALTO

T.C.

BASS

B.C.

continued

HIGH SCHOOL MIXED CHORUS

BOYS' CHOIR
(Trained Boy-Sopranos)

CHILDREN
(Boys & Girls - Untrained)

SUPPLEMENTARY INSTRUMENTS

AUTOHARP (12 CHORD)

T.C.
& B.C.

CHORD BARS

Gm B♭ A⁷ C⁷ Dm F E⁷ G⁷ Am C D⁷ G

CIMBALON (Dulcimer)
Fr. Tympanon;
It. Cembalon, Cimbalom or Cembalo;
Ger. Hackbrett

T.C.
& B.C.

THEREMIN

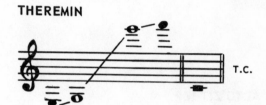

T.C.

MUSETTE (*2-PIPE BAGPIPE*)

T.C.

HIGHLAND BAGPIPE

CHANTER

(sounds approx.
¼ tone sharp)

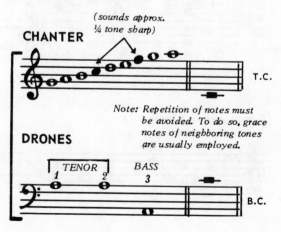

T.C.

Note: Repetition of notes must
be avoided. To do so, grace
notes of neighboring tones
are usually employed.

HANDBELLS

T.C.

DRONES

TENOR   BASS

B.C.

continued

ZITHERS

ZITHER (Treble & Concert)
Fr. Zither;
It. Zittera;
Ger. Schlagzither, Primzither
(Treble Zither),
(Concert Zither)

Melody Strings

Accompaniment Strings
As Written - Sound 8va basso

ALTO ZITHER
Fr. Zither Alto;
It. Zittera Alto;
Ger. Elegie, Alt or Liederzither

Melody Strings

Accompaniment Strings
As Written - Sound 8va basso

* *Alternate Tuning*

FRENCH

ITALIAN

Accordeon, 23.
Arpa, 44-48.
Arpicordo (Clavicembalo), 24.
Baritono, 54.
Baritono Basso, 54.
Basso, 54.
Campane (Campanelle), 18.
Campanelle (Campane), 18.
Campanetta, 18.
Chitarra, 19.
Clarinetto, 6, 7.
Clarino Contrabasso, 7.
Clarone, 7.
Clavicembalo (Arpicordo), 24.
Clavicordo, 24.
Contrabasso, 22.
Contrafagotto, 4.
Contralto, 54.
Cornetta (Cornetto), 11.
Cornetto (Cornetta), 11.
Corno di Bassetto, 7.
Corno Inglese, 4.
Corno Ventile, 14.
Eufonio, 17.
Fagotto, 4.
Flauto, 3.
Flauto Dolce, 52.
Flautone, 3.
Flicorno, 11.
Flicorno Tenore, 17.
Liuto, 53.
Mandolino, 20.
Mezzo Soprano, 54.
Organo, 25-39.

Ottavino, 3.
Pianoforte, 23.
Piffero, 3.
Sarrusofone, 5.
Sassophone, 8.
Soprano, 54.
Tenore, 54.
Timpani, 18.
Tromba, 9, 10, 12.
Vibrafono, 18.
Viola, 22.
Violino, 22.
Violoncello, 22
Zilafone, 18.
Zittera, 58.

GERMAN

MEMORANDUM